Praise for *Small Change: Great Impact!*

—∭—

"This book is a spiritual awakening. It makes you think about your life, your family, and your relationships. It also poses the question, "What are you doing to make things right? The language of the book is applicable to the common man as well as the educated. Most importantly, it also applies to women. Women can use the book to become better mothers, wives, daughters, sisters, and friends. *Small Change: Great Impact!* helps you to envision the love God has for you and makes you want to do something different in terms of improving the quality of your relationship with Him. This book gives you concrete examples and words of encouragement that can lead to change. Reading the book will lead to self- examination and awareness of your spiritual relationship and how this can be used to improve yourself and other relationships. You will be enlightened, encouraged, and inspired to become a better Christian."

—Stacia Davis Hill, Ph.D., HSPP
Counseling psychologist

"This book is a must-read for every man! Pastor Darryl understands the plight of our men, especially African American men. This book is not only a diagnosis of our pain but a remedy for our problems!"

—Pastor Terry A. Webster Sr.,
NU Corinthian Baptist Church

"Today we are overwhelmed by statistics concerning men dropping out of high school, missing out on college and the family, abusive in relationships, participating in more and more criminal activity and bored with the church. God is using Pastor Darryl Webster to spark a revolution that is reviving and restoring men to take back their God-given leadership roles in the home and church. The *Christian Men Connect (Boot Camp)* experience provides men with biblical principles in which practical applications are interwoven with small-group fellowship, prayer and public testimony.

In this inspiring book, *Small Change: Great Impact!*, Pastor Webster shares with the rest of the body of Christ what God is doing at Emmanuel Missionary Baptist Church. This is a testimonial of the amazing work of God through the Bible in the lives of men. Pastor Webster desires to "help inspire men of the local church to experience God at a deeper level by encouraging them to take a 21-day journey with the Lord." In the book he walks you through the various stations in *Boot Camp*. Each station is designed to transform men into spiritual leaders freed from the bondage of sin. Testimonies of salvation and victory over enslaving sin habits document how paralyzing despair can be replaced with liberating hope.

Anyone interested in a practical local church-oriented men's program centered around the Man, Jesus Christ, need to read *Small Change: Great Impact!*"

—A. Charles Ware, D.D.
President, Crossroads Bible College

"This book is timely, practical and biblical! Pastor Webster has modeled a guide to empower men to truly become the men God has called them to be. These changes will be experienced by everyone they encounter."

—Janice Adams, MSW, ACSW, LSW
Associate Professor, Director Social Work Education
Indiana Wesleyan University
Part-Time Therapist – Domestic Violence
Family Service Society

Small Change: Great Impact!

A Journey of Deliverance for Christian Men

—⚊⚊⚊—

by

Darryl K. Webster

Foreword by Dr. Lloyd C. Blue

—ɯɯ—

This book is dedicated to my wife, Sibyl, and my children—Quincy, Darrin, Kristin, and Kelli—for encouraging me to be the husband and father that God would have me to be and to the Emmanuel Missionary Baptist Church family and the men of Boot Camp for allowing me to lead and strengthen them as soldiers in God's army. Thanks for all of your love and support. Special thanks to Renee Bacon, Blonnie Burroughs, Serena Macklin and Stacia Hill for helping to bring this book together.

With this, my first book, I want to express my love and appreciation to others who have inspired, shaped and enriched my life and helped make me who I am today:

My Mother: Helen Webster
My Father: Jimmie Webster
My eight brothers and four sisters
The late Rev. Ananais Robinson
New Light Baptist Church family

Meet the Author
Pastor Darryl K. Webster
Servant, Preacher, Teacher

—∿∿—

Darryl K. Webster is the fervent pastor of Emmanuel Missionary Baptist Church in Indianapolis, Indiana. He is the husband of Sister Sibyl and the father of four children: Quincy, Kristin, Darrin and Kelli.

Pastor Webster received his calling in October 1983 and was ordained on November 24, 1985 at New Light Baptist Church in Indianapolis, Indiana. On March 31, 1996, Rev. Darryl K. Webster was installed as the pastor of Emmanuel Missionary Baptist Church in Indianapolis, Indiana.

Pastor Webster is a graduate of Martin University with a Master's degree in Urban Ministries and a Bachelor's degree in Religious Studies. His work in Urban Ministries has been so profound that in May 2008, he was inducted into the Martin University Alumni Hall of Fame in recognition of his efforts.

Pastor Webster serves as an adjutant professor at Crossroads Bible College. He is a certified instructor for "Proclaiming the Word Ministries," as well as programs for awareness and prevention of STD's and AIDS in the African American community. Pastor Webster is the founder and CEO of Emmanuel Preparatory Academy, which provides

Christian child care for the church body and community. Previously, he served as the chaplain of the IUPUI Basketball Team. Pastor Webster also is one of the founders of the "Sharpening Your Tools Conference."

Pastor Webster is a highly requested facilitator for conducting single's conferences, family crisis conferences, marriage seminars and church revivals. His preaching ministry is known throughout the Midwest as well as in Ghana, West Africa, where his sermons are broadcasted and his church financially supports two churches, a blind school and a technical school.

Pastor Webster believes in a holistic ministry. He and the Emmanuel Missionary Baptist Church family appear regularly on the local Christian television station, TBN). He strives to instill into his congregation that all believers must first love God and then serve God by reaching out to others, exhibiting Christ's love in action with daily deeds.

Contents

—⟋⟋⟋—

Foreword

—∿∿—

No other book does what this one does so well. All men, whether they are single, married and/or fathers, no matter what walk of life they are from, will be blessed by this book. At the invitation of Reverend Darryl Webster, I have witnessed first hand the kind of spiritual revival that can come to a group of men exposed to this Spiritual Boot Camp strategy: A little change will surely produce a great impact.

I sat through two sessions of the 21-day Boot Camp in October 2007 at the Emmanuel Church, pastored by the author. Each morning as I arrived at 5:00, I saw men running across the parking lot to experience God and His awesome power. As these same men entered the sanctuary, they were singing and shouting in the aisles. While God began to work in the lives of those men gathered, I heard them confess their sin in tears and plead for prayer. I also heard them cry out to God, asking Him to fill them with the Holy Spirit.

Using biblical principles, Reverend Webster teaches them how to become Christian men of character and integrity. He is a true champion for Christ. I love him as a father loves his son. Just talking to him gives you a sense of purpose. Reverend Webster has provided us with a tool to encourage a small change that is sure to have a great impact.

We, the church leadership, namely the pastor, must work diligently to disciple the men of the church and train them so that they can train others (2 Timothy 2:2). I believe thousands of pastors are going to realize what a tremendous tool this book is and use it to help the men in their churches and communities. Now you know why I am so excited about this book, *Small Change: Great Impact!* What a helpful resource—full of examples and great spiritual guidance. I believe this book will help anyone to have an exciting Spirit-filled life.

—Dr. Lloyd C. Blue
Founder/President
Church Growth Unlimited, Inc.

Preface:

It's All About Change

—∿—

In 2002, I started working out with an exercise regimen to build my temple for the Lord and help prolong my health. I joined the local YMCA. My cardio routine on the treadmill initially began with a half mile to a mile, which increased to one to three miles. After a while, I was able to stay on the treadmill for three to four miles, and then I progressed to four to six miles. This regimen helped to prepare and equip me to not only participate in, but successfully complete, two mini- marathons. Imagine that! I made a small change to my daily routine by incorporating a regular exercise program, and, to my utter amazement, my body began to do more for me than it ever had.

Marathons are not for the meek or timid. A commitment must be made, followed by conditioning and training. As I ran the marathons, I saw several people who had made a small change leading to a great impact. I saw people who were old and slow, but they crossed the finish line. I saw people who were overweight; yet, their commitment to a small change allowed them to run stronger and fast enough to beat my finish time.

There were also groups who ran that encouraged one another. A little encouragement can even make a great impact. The runners were dodging chuckholes and taking off layers of clothing during the race. They had discovered that even the smallest change can have a great impact. They were seeking to finish the race, and that's exactly what they did. What an impact on their personal lives!

The decision to take charge of my temple by exercising regularly would mean that I needed to discipline myself in other areas as well. As much as I loved fried foods like chicken and catfish, I had to make a small change in my eating habits. Discipline would also mean that I needed to get a good night's sleep. I am amazed at what a small change did in my life and what it can do in the lives of others.

This is an example of a small change with great *physical* impact. One may also commit to a small change that will result in a great *spiritual* impact that is equally life altering. Allow the book in hand, *Small Change: Great Impact!* to take you on a journey of deliverance that is sure to change your life and those around you.

Small Change

—ɯ—

Your life is filled with opportunities for making small
positive changes. When you look for them, you'll see
those opportunities in every direction.
Even one small change can have a large positive impact
on your life because the benefits of that small change are
repeated day after day. Keep adding more small positive
changes from time to time, and the results
can be truly incredible.
Give yourself the gift today of a small positive change in
your life. And continue to enjoy the rewards you receive
far into the future.

—Ralph Marston, *DailyMotivator.com*

Introduction

—⟋⟍—

Small Change: Great Impact! was written to help inspire men of their local churches to experience God at a deeper level by encouraging them to take a 21-day journey with the Lord. Far too often, Christian men have felt a disconnection and discontentment in their relationship with Christ. As a result, many have no motivation to go higher or deeper in their pilgrimage with Him. This book is designed to help men reconnect with the Lord and feel good about their relationship with Him, as well as their service to Him.

In the pages that lie ahead, it is my intent to inspire or encourage a small change in the lives of men that, with the Holy Spirit's help, will have a great impact. If we men would just make a small investment in our spiritual lives, God will give us a great dividend in return. It is not how much time we have to live; but more importantly, it's what we *do* during the time we live.

Imagine what would happen if men made a small change in their spiritual lives. It would improve their relationship with God and help them master their disabilities and hang-ups. It would carry over into their relationships with their wives, children, and others.

This life-changing experience, which I have termed Christian Men Connect, can be compared to a man going to the doctor's office for a physical. The doctor will often check his blood pressure, perform an EKG of his heart, and take a sample of his blood for analysis. Before he leaves the office, the doctor is able to give him the results of the blood pressure test, indicating whether it is high or low. He will also give him the results of his EKG, noting whether the news is good or bad. Yet, his blood work still has to be sent off to a lab, and a follow-up appointment must be scheduled in order to receive those results.

Once the doctor assesses his physical condition, he may determine that he has a need for a prescription to treat the problem. The doctor will recommend that the patient take the medication for a certain length of time while he monitors his condition. If his condition does not improve with the medication and care he has recommended, he will refer him to a specialist; so it is with the spiritual condition of many Christian men.

The 21-day Christian boot camp for men, Christian Men Connect, is like being under the doctor's care so that he may monitor and treat your spiritual condition. The stations that you will visit in the Spiritual Boot Camp are designed to help you search your soul and see yourself in the light of the Word of God.

So often, we attend and conduct men's conferences and programs during which the speaker addresses and tackles some very tough issues. As men, we may even open up once we have been made aware of those issues. Many times, however, we return home with no relevant or practical solutions to handle our problems. Even when we are given solutions, there is no one available to hold us accountable. This book will give you helpful solutions to address these pertinent problems and hold yourself accountable as well.

When I accepted Jesus Christ into my life, I was 16 years old. It was a crisis moment, but the flame that He lit in this poor boy from a family of 13 siblings has kept, changed, empowered and convicted me, along with setting me free. For over 27 years, the Lord has been making Himself known to me through the Bible and many life experiences. I can recall time after time when I have needed direction about life, marriage and jobs. Every time, without fail, the Lord has given me a word through the Bible or His preacher. For a poor boy growing up in a dysfunctional family and sometimes struggling with low self-esteem, this was and is of the most importance. Who I am right now at this stage of my life is only because of my Lord and Savior.

> *Something supernatural occurs when men get right with God.*

Let me encourage you as a pastor and leader of men to commit yourself to lead the men in your church on this journey and watch God transform their lives. At my church, the experience was so electrifying that the women started talking and testifying about the changes that they witnessed in the lives of their husbands and sons. The impact was so great that they wanted to present them with a medal of adoration for their commitment to God. *Praise the Lord!* Most important, the church was spiritually impacted in a way I have never experienced since I have been a Christian. Something supernatural occurs when men get right with God.

> *Unfortunately, there appears to be a great disconnect with the people of God from the power of God in the church today.*

Unfortunately, there appears to be a great disconnect with the people of God from the power of God in the church today. Many believers have become cloudy and cool, as well as casual and comfortable with their lackadaisical spiritual lives. This attitude and behavior leaves them uncommitted and unwilling to go any deeper in their walk with God.

Over the years, I have watched so many Christians become dissatisfied with their unhealthy spiritual lives because of addictions and other bondages that hinder their spiritual growth, thus causing them to repeatedly fall prey to the Devil's web of deceit. The Lord convicted me as a shepherd to let me know I had to do something more than the normal or regular routine to help His sheep.

After praying and steadfastly seeking God, He placed this vision of Christian Men Connect in my heart to help men come face to face with God and themselves. For the 21 days that were to follow, God ignited a fire that is still burning. Out of all my 27 years as a Christian and 12 years in the pastorate, I have never experienced the power of God in such a phenomenal, transformational way.

It is very encouraging to look back today and offer a sober reflection of what transpired at Emmanuel Missionary Baptist Church in the month of October 2006. So may God be glorified, and may you and every man in your sphere of life experience the awesome and transformational power of God at work in you.

Remember to evaluate your spiritual growth at the end of each station, being mindful that any small change in you has the potential to make a big impact in every area of your life and the lives of others. The men touched by this experience will never be the same. May this book challenge men to make a small positive change. I am confident that you will be amazed at the great impact it will make.

—Pastor Darryl K. Webster

Spiritual Boot Camp

—∞—

Finally, my brethren, be strong in the Lord, and in the power of His might, put on the whole armor of God that ye may be able to stand against the wiles of the devil...Praying always with all prayers and supplication in the spirit, and watching thereunto with all perseverance and supplication for all saints.
—Ephesians 6:10-18

Why "Spiritual Boot Camp" *for men*? Statistics show that men are under attack. There are several battles that Christian men face daily. They battle with issues that negatively impact their health, family and overall quality of life spent here on earth. When you look at the startling statistics surrounding men, our only hope is spiritual intervention.

The statistics regarding men and HIV/AIDS are startling. Until There's a Cure reports that of the 40,000 new HIV/AIDS cases, 70 percent are men. According to the Center for Disease Control, at all stages of HIV/AIDS—from infection with HIV to death with AIDS—African Americans greatly outnumber members of other races and ethnicities. According to the 2000 census, African Americans represented 13% of the U.S. population. However, in 2005, African Americans accounted for 18,121 (49%) of the estimated 37,331 new HIV/AIDS diagnoses in the United States in the 33 states that have long-term, confidential name-based HIV reporting. *Men's Health* tells us that the health of African American men is far worse than any other racial group, which is evident in the statistic that they live 7.1 years less than these same comparison groups. How can men head their families if they are not healthy enough to do so?

The 2005 National Center for Health Statistics reports that 48 percent of all marriages end in divorce. Understanding that divorce contributes to the increase of single-parent homes, we must look at the impact on society. According to Rock New Haven Statistics, men from fatherless homes account for 71 percent of high school dropouts, 85 percent of behavior disorders, and 75 percent of adolescents in chemical abuse centers among other negative statistics.

What else can we learn from statistics regarding the family? The U.S. Department of Health & Human Services Healthy Marriage Initiative states that African Americans have lower rates of marriage and marital stability than all other ethnic groups. They also have higher rates of single-headed families when compared to other groups. The report goes on to say that African American individuals are more likely to be unmarried, divorced, or separated than any other race or ethnic group. The family as a unit is failing.

The quality of life can't be great if your life is being spent in incarceration. The Associated Press reported that one in 75 men is incarcerated. Of those incarcerated, racial and ethnic minorities make up 68 percent. Rock New Haven statistics also show that for every 100 women age 18-21 in correctional institutions, there are 1,430 men of the same age group in correctional institutions. That number of men increased for ages 22-24 to 1,448.

Again, these statistics are startling but not impossible to turn around with God's help. There is an all-out assault against men; and if we don't use spiritual tactics to address the issues, we will continue to see these depressing numbers plague our families, communities, and nation.

This spiritual boot camp will dig deep to the root of problems facing men and open the door to deliverance. As with military boot camp, two crucial basics of Christian life must be practiced every day until they become a part of every man's spiritual make-up. We must repent daily and commit to building a personal relationship with God.

> *Although we know that repentance and confession comes at the hour of salvation, it is also required in our daily walk with the Lord.*

Early in our Christian walk, we learn that confession is good for the soul but is often misinterpreted as a sign of weakness. On the contrary, confession is not a sign of weakness but a mark of strength. Acknowledgement of sin is powerful because it begins the healing process. Once you see men break down and openly confess to defiling the temple of God through deliberate sinful activity and practices, you can truly say that this spiritual boot camp, Christian Men Connect, was and is God at work. It is Him righting the wrong in His children. Although we know that repentance and confession comes at the hour of salvation, it is also required in our daily walk with the Lord.

> *A good or positive relationship with God ...preparing us for a victorious outcome in the battles we will face.*

The Ephesians passage heading up this chapter, "Spiritual Boot Camp," reminds us that once we become born-again believers, we are instantly in a battle. Therefore, it is always refreshing to pause during our busy schedule to share the blessings and joy of the Lord and get closer to Him. It is also our responsibility to constantly strengthen our relationship with our Creator. A good or positive relationship with God ultimately overflows into our everyday lives—including our family, friends and neighbors—preparing us for a victorious outcome in the battles we will face.

The men who attended Christian Men Connect were there to strengthen their relationship with God and interface with the Lord Jesus Christ in order to draw closer to Him, experience Him, and hear from Him. They were also there to reflect on and improve their family lives, job interactions, and areas of struggle and weakness. Some who attended came out of sheer curiosity. Whatever their purposes may have been, the men made a commitment to show up, and that's exactly what they did. It was evident in the parking lot each morning at 5:30.

The vertical commitment with God was followed by a horizontal commitment with those who gathered together. The men took their commitment to another level by signing a privacy covenant, which helped them remove their masks by creating a level of comfort and security. Through this covenant, the men vowed that what was said in boot camp would stay in boot camp. If someone was found sharing each other's stories without their permission, they risked being removed from the group. We agreed, however, that we could share one another's stories without revealing their names. The level of trust grew, and we became **brothers**. Take a look at the commitment we made to one another.

Boot Camp
Confidentiality Covenant

Because of other's testimonies, Christ answered my prayers.

"Boot Camp" is our metaphor that depicts the need for specialized discipleship training for life. Just as soldiers prepare for battle, godly men must prepare for the challenges of life. Through discipline, community, and accountability, God equips us to conquer our challenges. During Christian Men Connect, men will be encouraged to nurture their spiritual lives, process complex issues, and engage in small-group community fellowship.

The vertical commitment to God must be followed by a horizontal commitment with the men (brothers) gathered. Genesis 24 shows me that God swears in His servants to their work—that having sworn, they may perform it.

I, the undersigned, make a solemn vow before God to hold the personal matters disclosed in this boot camp in the strictest confidence. I love my brothers and will not divulge anything I have heard to anyone. I enter into this covenant with my community of brothers, trusting God to make us better men. I will keep my brothers before God in my prayers.

Signature   *Date*

I knew that the covenant would be critical throughout the 21 days when it came to the depth of confessions and testimonies ahead. We staged seven different workstations to visit daily for a time of sharing, teaching and experiencing God. But what the Lord did was far greater than what anyone, including myself, could ever imagine.

Having said that, I'm sure the religious skeptics may question the spiritual relevance of boot camp by saying it is not biblical for men to be compelled or persuaded to leave their family and sacrifice sleep, time and gas to be at the church at such an early hour. On the contrary, the Bible refers to a spiritual exercise similar to Christian Men Connect. The prophet Daniel organized all-night prayer meetings with the young Hebrew lads to seek the face of God for an answer to a threat of death (Daniel 2:14-19). Daniel, as a spiritual leader, knew that it would take more than ordinary daily prayers to get certain answers from God.

I want to give you more than just my outlook on this spiritual journey of deliverance. Take a look at this personal account which one brother wrote on his thoughts and experiences at our 21-day boot camp. He is a missionary from Ghana, West Africa, who happened to be visiting the United States.

I am a Witness!

When I first heard of boot camp, I was curious as to what it was all about. The military term seemed strange and did not stretch my imagination, much more my thoughts. I literally had no foreknowledge of this soul- searching, Spirit-filled exercise or its relationship to boot camp.

It was in Ghana that I would serve as a one-time member of the cadet corps and get a first-hand experience into this "boot camp" idea. While participating in Christian Men Connect, I was reminded of the intense discipline involved and strenuous daily routines I endured as a cadet in Ghana.

Every day in the Ghana Cadet Corps, including Sunday, the sergeant-major would issue a command at 4:00 a.m. Each cadet was urged to "fall in" as commanded. There was an expectation to take between five to 10 minutes to shower, dress and report at the parade grounds for special instructions. It was a test of strength and commitment that was not to be taken lightly.

If you routinely slept until 6:00 a.m., you had to make an adjustment when you joined the cadet corps. Wake-up time was much earlier in order to make the 4:00 a.m. command call. It was a big sacrifice that instilled discipline as well as physical fitness. When it was time to do push-ups or run a marathon, you dared not to be left behind. Your punishment would be worse than what you endured during the training exercise. Many began the first few days optimistic about their capabilities until they found out that they were not prepared, or better yet, they had not psyched up well enough for what was ahead.

The training exercises of the Christian Men Connect Spiritual Boot Camp were just as trying as those in the Ghana Cadet Corps. I must say that it was all worth it. I watched my brothers fight battles that they could have never fought alone. The exercises strengthened us physically, mentally and spiritually. This experience led me to ponder how this same concept could be used at my church in Ghana as a tool to effectively reach the men. Never would I have imagined the impact this would have on my life.

> *It is always amazing how the power of God can stir up the hearts of men who have undertaken the path of repentance and seek spiritual restitution.*

Christian Men Connect gave an opportunity for every man in attendance to critically examine himself and allow the Holy Spirit to reveal his true self. After which, the Holy Spirit could help change every man for the better through confession of any open or secret sin. It is always amazing how the power of God can stir up the hearts of men who have undertaken the path of repentance and seek spiritual restitution.

This 21-day journey sought to do something daring and radical to get answers from God, just as Daniel and his friends did. *Christian men, this is a war cry!* **Man Up** and get properly prepared and equipped for a victorious battle.

Reflect and Respond

Often, it is hard to get Christian men to be real and follow other men for one day; it's hard to imagine 21. As you have read the opening part of this book, you should know that what God has done in the lives of these men and how He has used me as a pastor is possible for you as well. God is no respecter of persons, and He is able to do the impossible in and through you if you would only let Him. Start praying with urgency like Daniel. Pray not only for yourself but for your fellow brothers. Be willing to allow the Holy Spirit to convict, challenge, encourage and lead you on this personal journey to become a better husband, father, brother, son and man. Reclaim your position and take your place, my brother. God has great things in store for you!

1. What do you expect to receive from reading *Small Change: Great Impact!*?

---

2. How is your connection with God? What may be causing any type of disconnection?

---

3. As a men's leader or layperson, have you taken the path of repentance to seek spiritual restitution?

_____

_____

4. How are you preparing or equipping yourself for a victorious battle?

_____

_____

5. Give the name of at least one other man that you would like to see God move mightily in his life.

_____

_____

5:45 a.m.

—ळ—

And all the people came early in the morning to hear him
at the temple. —Luke 21:38 (NIV)

Only God Himself could have orchestrated the Spirit-filled gathering that occurred at 5:45 a.m. for 21 days at "the church in the valley with a mountain top experience and message" as some 100 men from various walks of life—young, old, rich, poor, married, single, divorced, educated, professionals, ex-felons, community leaders, entrepreneurs, new converts, veteran saints, grandfathers, fathers and sons—began arriving from all points of the city. They arrived walking, riding bicycles and carpooling; some were even dropped off to gather at what one would have thought was a major sporting event.

The men eagerly entered the church sanctuary as sacred music played softly in the background. The music set the atmosphere and tone for an encounter that few men had ever witnessed: a mighty move of God through what became known as Boot Camp—Christian Men Connect. Close your eyes, take a deep breath and picture men literally rushing into the church to pray and experience the supernatural power of God. Breathtaking!

The brisk winds of fall or other bad weather conditions, heavy workloads, hectic schedules, lack of sleep, school assignments, family problems nor personal responsibilities would be enough to hinder or interfere with the men's bold determination to go on a journey of deliverance that would lead to change and positive impact. (You have already envisioned the arrival of the men. Now let me take you inside to witness the spiritual healing begin.)

The men were divided into five different groups called *squads*. The squads were led by either a squad leader or servant leader. These leaders were responsible for the daily reports of their assigned men. The level of accountability was extremely high. The men had to inform their leaders if or when they were going to be absent. If they did not make contact, their absence was considered unexcused. The leader excused an absence if they were notified. On the other hand, if a man was absent and did not contact his leader for three consecutive days, he was considered AWOL (absent without leave).

Like clockwork, a few men would stand before those assembled, leading them in a time of devotion with song, Scriptures, prayer and testimony. This initial connection to God was the perfect fuel to get the day started! You could feel the intensity of the presence of God in our midst as we joined hands in a big circle, praying out loud and at other times silently. The men were unified as they gathered to connect with God and reach out to one another.

Surely, no real soldier ever goes into battle without knowing how to use his weapon effectively. The books of the Bible were memorized to help the brothers learn how to handle their weapon.

Similar to military protocol, one of the "spiritual" officers stood boldly, calling the men to attention as the morning drills and mental gymnastics exercises were performed. The exercises consisted of a review of the Word of the day, as well as a recitation of the books of the Bible and assigned Bible verses from memory. Surely, no real soldier ever goes into battle without knowing how to use his weapon effectively. The books of the Bible were memorized to help the brothers learn how to handle their weapon.

It is sad to see Christians fumbling through pages of the Bible, unable to find Scriptures because they cannot handle their weapon. I'm happy to report that before boot camp was over, the men were not only able to learn all the books of the Bible but recite them in order as well. This recitation and the other spiritual drills were very powerful and important, but they were not the purpose of our gathering.

With hearts and minds eternally focused under my leadership and instruction, the men formed an orderly procession and marched to the upper level of the sanctuary, singing in adoration choruses of *"He is Lord."* Excitement was in the air as we all made our way to the work stations. Equipped with a Bible in one hand and a notebook in the other, we were attentive and alert. All of us were uncertain of what was ahead, but we were eager to hear and see how God would reveal Himself to us, both personally and corporately.

+-----------------------+ _____
| |
| ***Reflect*** |
| ***and*** |
| ***Respond*** |
| |
+-----------------------+

Our Lord and Savior Jesus Christ called His followers and made them disciples. While discipling them, He taught them the need to pray as told to us in the Book of Luke: "And He spake a parable unto them to this end, that men ought always to pray, and not to faint" (Luke 18:1). The apostle John spoke of the need for fellowship and explained how it can be accomplished in his book, 1 John. He confronted the issue of our character when he stated, "If we say that we have fellowship with Him and walk in darkness, we lie, and do not the truth: but if we walk in the light, as He is in the light, we have fellowship one with another, and the blood of Jesus Christ His Son cleanseth us from all sin" (1 John 1:6-7 KJV). The apostle John also cautioned us when he said, If we say that we have no sin, we deceive ourselves and the truth is not in us. If we confess our sins He is faithful and just to forgive us our sins, and to cleanse us from all unrighteousness *(1 John 1:8-9).*

1. Read the above passage. How important do you think prayer and fellowship are to God? Does your character reflect this?

_____

_____

2. What do you feel keeps men from not praying or fellow-
    shipping consistently with other men?

    _____

    _____

3. Are you prepared to make a commitment to become a
    better Christian, even if you must sacrifice by losing
    sleep, allowing your schedule to be disrupted, waking up
    early, leaving your family for 21 days, etc.?

    _____

    _____

4. Do you think you have what it takes to be an active
    member of a spiritual boot camp or would you, like so
    many others, drop out or go AWOL?

    _____

    _____

5. How well do you handle your spiritual weapon, the
    Bible? Are you fully prepared for war?

    _____

    _____

Man Up! Bow Down

—ɯɯ—

*By humility and the fear of the LORD are riches,
and honour, and life.* —Proverbs 22:4

Station 1: *Humility*

Station One was "Humility." The word literally means, "he who bends himself." The Scripture passage we spent a large amount of time focusing on was James 4:6 (NKJV) that recounts, *But He gives more grace. Therefore He says: "God resists the proud, but gives grace to the humble."* Even though humility is not a part of the average Christian man's make-up, it was my goal to help the men examine themselves and see their need to humble themselves before God. According to Psalm 51:17, *The sacrifices of God are a broken spirit: a broken and a contrite heart, O God, thou wilt not despise.* We discussed how God absolutely opposes the proud. The men were challenged to let go of their egos and take off the masks that they were so accustomed to wearing.

The brothers were also reminded that they could not experience God fully with an attitude of pride. We then read a very convicting passage of Scripture, Proverbs 6:16-19 (NKJV), which says, *These six things the Lord hates, yes, seven are an abomination to Him: a proud look, a lying tongue, hands that shed innocent blood, a heart that devises wicked plans, feet that are swift in running to evil, a false witness who speaks lies, and one who sows discord among brethren.*

It was vital for the men to understand how God views pride and the outcome of arrogance: *Pride goes before destruction and a haughty spirit before a fall* (Proverbs 16:18). They needed to know that a fall— sometimes of great magnitude—was inevitable if they did not face their short-comings or deal with them, whether they involved pride or any other behavior that displeased God.

I realize, however, that not everyone is arrogant. You may just need to make a decision to submit to the will of God if you haven't already taken that step. Station Two will take you deeper and explain about that level of submission.

After listening to the Word and looking intently and honestly within ourselves, we began to acknowledge our shortcomings. This was very powerful, and at times, extraordinary. There were over 50 men kneeling before the Lord at the same time. Our prayers to the Lord included a plea for forgiveness and help to overcome our shortcomings. Above all, we prayed that He would help us yield to His will for our lives. As the power of prayer began to move, it was no surprise to see men crying and willingly sharing their testimonies regarding how the Lord had humbled them.

Of several testimonies told, I will only share a few. One businessman shared with us about the pain he is still experiencing to this day due to God's humbling process. All of his time and finances had gone into his business. He had placed earthly riches above God and his family, and he was no longer focused on God's business but his own personal financial gain. As a Christian, he was well aware of the promises of God and that heavenly treasures far exceed any riches here on earth.

Yet, how quickly the ground beneath him began to tremble. His spiritual and family life suffered. His marriage was strained, and his finances were unstable—all because he took his eyes off of God. As a "good" businessman, he confessed how hard it was to accept what God was doing as he humbled himself before God.

Another man shared that his priorities were not aligned with God's. He admitted that God told him he smelled of pride, and that odor was not at all pleasing to Him. In the past, he had felt invincible. Yet, his mother became ill, and he could not understand why this and other circumstances were happening in his life. He later realized that it was God trying to get his attention. God knew that the only way to reach him was by helping him get his priorities straight. First, however, he had to let go of pride and humble himself before God.

We encouraged the men to choose to become humble on their own before the Lord forced it upon them. Let's look at King Nebuchadnezzar:

> *All this came upon the king Nebuchadnezzar. At the end of twelve months he walked in the palace of the kingdom of Babylon. The king spake, and said, Is not this great Babylon, that I have built for the hours of the kingdom by the might of my power, and for the honour of my majesty? While the word was in the king's mouth, there fell a voice from heaven, saying, O king Nebuchadnezzar, to thee it is spoken; the kingdom is departed from thee. And they shall drive thee from men, and thy dwelling shall be with the beasts of the field: they shall make thee to eat grass as oxen, and seven times shall pass over thee, until thou know that the most High ruleth in the kingdom of men, and giveth it to whomsoever He will. The same hour was the thing fulfilled upon Nebuchadnezzar: and he was driven from men, and did eat grass as oxen. . . " (Daniel 4:28-33).*

It was an enlightening moment at Station One as we came face to face with *self* and acknowledged our shortcomings to God. Dealing with our pride was a major hurdle, but we were able to understand our issues and help hold one another accountable. Having done so, we could now proceed to face the next 20 days. We were ready because we had told God all about ourselves—the good, the bad and the ugly.

> *The only ray of hope in man's spiritual darkness is the sovereign grace of God.*

Reflecting on what happened to Nebuchadnezzar is very sobering; however, James said that God would give grace to the humble. Hallelujah! Aren't you, like me, glad about that? The only ray of hope in man's spiritual darkness is the sovereign grace of God. His grace alone can cause man to withdraw from his propensity to lust for evil things and deliver him from self. God's granting of "more grace" shows that His grace is greater than the power of sin, the flesh, the world and Satan (Romans 5:20-21).

> *A truly humble person will give his allegiance to God, obey His commands and follow His leadership.*

Both Proverbs 3:34 in the Old Testament and I Peter 5:5 reveal who can obtain God's grace. Both verses state that it is the humble who receives grace, not the proud. The proud are enemies of God. According to the Scriptures, the term "humble" does not signify a special class of Christians, but instead should refer to all believers. (See Isaiah 57:15, 66:2; and Matthew 18:3-4.) A truly humble person will give his allegiance to God, obey His commands and follow His leadership.

The men had completed Station One, pondering what the Lord would do next. Well, just as in the military, since this was spiritual boot camp, I introduced them and moved quickly to the next station.

Reflect and Respond

Don't allow your pride, ego and selfish ambition to take you down a dangerous road God never intended for you to go, just to get to a place or position you think you should be. Wait in humble submission as He places you according to His will, way and time. Remember, Father knows best! *For whosoever exalteth himself shall be abased; and he that humbleth himself shall be exalted* (Luke 14:11).

1. Do you have any areas of pride that you have not come face to face with? Stop right now and talk to God about them.

   _____

   _____

2. Are you experiencing God fully? If not, ask Him to show you why and be willing to accept His response.

   _____

   _____

3. Re-read Proverbs 6:16-19. Why do you think the Lord put pride first on His hate list?

_____

_____

4. List your top three shortcomings. Then ask a relative or friend who will be very truthful to do the same. See how your lists compare and contrast.

_____

_____

5. As a believer, you can obtain God's grace. Are you taking advantage of this privilege as a grateful recipient or does pride stand in the way?

_____

_____

Fall In Line

—ᴍᴍ—

"He that findeth his life shall lose it; and he that loseth his life for my sake shall find it." —Matthew 10:39

Station 2: *Submission*

Station Two was our "Submission" station. After humbling ourselves and surrendering to the will of God, it was time to dive deeper. James 4:7 says to "Submit yourselves therefore to God." To submit means "to line up under." This word was used to describe soldiers under the authority of their commander. The New Testament describes Jesus' submission to His parents' authority (Luke 2:51), the Church's submission to Christ (Ephesians 5:24) and servants' submission to their masters (Titus 2:9; 1 Peter 2:18). James uses the word to denote a willing, conscious submission to God's authority as sovereign ruler of the universe.

In Matthew 10:39, Jesus was demanding total commitment from His disciples; this commitment even extended to physical death. It also made the call to full surrender a part of the message the disciples were to proclaim to others.

One of the hardest things to do is getting men to submit or surrender their life to the lordship of Jesus Christ without taking the control back from Him the next minute or day. We habitually submit ourselves to other things like our jobs, sports, education, family and our own selfish desires; but we do not submit ourselves fully to God. We must realize that God will not continue to take second place because He is a jealous God (Exodus 20:5).

Submission is a fundamental attitude linked with spiritual maturity.

> *The lack of submission to the Lord makes life difficult and can cause us to miss out on God's purpose for our lives.*

The lack of submission to the Lord makes life difficult and can cause us to miss out on God's purpose for our lives. Our own disobedience can also delay His plan for our lives. When we are deliberate about falling in line with God, He knows we are serious and will help us. We encouraged the brothers to make an intentional decision to submit themselves to the Lord, according to His Word.

To close out the "Submission" station, we bowed down on our knees together before God, lifting our hands up to heaven. With outstretched hands in submission to God, we recited the words of Jesus as He hung upon the cross: "Father, not My will, but Thy will be done." The men were then reminded that these are not just mere words to be quoted. They were willing to accept whatever God sent their way. For Jesus, it was the cross, but for us we just didn't know. This session concluded with an appeal to the men to renew their commitment to the Lord and make a choice to submit to Him daily.

This was such a hot topic that it compelled many of the men to express how they wrestled with submission. One brother shared that God had to send him to jail before he fully surrendered. He was alone and had no one to talk to during his sentence. Every day he looked for a letter from a family member or a friend, but there was nothing.

As he sat alone in his cell, he felt as though no one cared. He was down and out, feeling abandoned and alone. To his amazement there was a Bible within reach. He opened it and began to read. It was then that he discovered God loved him. He said at that moment he fell down on his knees and surrendered his life to the will of the Lord Jesus Christ. He learned that God has several ways to get you to submit.

Another brother shared how hard it was for him to live according to the Word of God and His will. He said that he had made several attempts to commit to the will of God, but he always found himself taking the reins back from Him. He stated how it had cost him money, heartaches, sleepless nights, and marital problems— all because he struggled with doing it God's way. He stated that the joy that comes when he's walking in the will of God and the peace that it brings when he submits to Him makes life worth living.

Reflect and Respond

In April 2007, our city participated in the nationally recognized program, Fugitive Safe Surrender (FSS). The program encourages persons who are wanted for non-violent felonies or misdemeanors to voluntarily surrender (note: submit) to faith-based leaders and law enforcement officers in faith institutions. The four-day initiative resulted in 531 individuals turning themselves in to the authorities for various reasons. Just as the individuals in this program, if you have not fully submitted and surrendered unto God, you are a Christian fugitive. The wonderful thing is God, too, has provided an opportunity for you to make a safe surrender. Stop making excuses, turn yourself in today and submit unto His Lordship.

1. What place is Christ in your life right now – first, second, or other?

_____

_____

2. Describe a time when you have been disobedient and done something your way and not God's.

_____

_____

3. In what area is the Devil enticing you which keeps you from submitting fully unto the Lord and fulfilling His plan and purpose for you?

    _____

    _____

4. Define submission in your own words.

    _____

    _____

5. What do you think causes men to struggle in the area of submission?

    _____

    _____

Take A Stand

—✵—

Lest Satan should get an advantage of us; for we are not ignorant of his devices. —2 Corinthians 2:11

Station Three: *Resist the Devil*

The apostle Paul said, *For we do not wrestle against flesh and blood, but against principalities, against powers, against the rulers of the darkness of this age, against spiritual hosts of wickedness in the heavenly places* (Ephesians 6:12 NKJV). I like what Henry Blackaby states: "In a battle, it is imperative to identify your enemy. If you are not aware of the point of your attack, you are vulnerable." The apostle Paul had many enemies; some resented him, many hated him, and others wanted to kill him. Some, who were supposedly on his side, sought to harm him and his ministry. (See Acts 9:23, Philippians 1:17, 2 Timothy 4:14.)

In spite of the persecution he faced, Paul never lost sight of his real enemy; he was wary of Satan. When people attacked him, he knew they were not his real opponents. They were simply unsuspecting instruments of the spiritual forces of darkness.

When you encounter opposition to your faith, your first reaction may be anger toward your adversary. This may divert your attention from the deeper spiritual dimensions of your conflict. Your enemy may be hopelessly in bondage to sin. Rather than retaliating, you should immediately and earnestly intercede for that person. Your opponent's hostility is your invitation to become involved in God's redemptive work to free him or her from spiritual bondage.

Be alert to the spiritual warfare around you. It is real and potentially destructive to you and those you care about. Knowing your real foe will protect you from bitterness and an unforgiving heart. Your hope lies in this reality: *He who is in you is greater than he who is in the world* (I John 4:4). Do not place your hope in people, but steadfastly trust in the One who has already defeated your enemy.

Station Three was devoted to strengthening the men to fight off the wiles of the Devil. At this station they were commissioned to resist the Devil at all times. We understand that this is not easy, but here is where we learned how. The word "resist" can be alternatively stated as, "stand your ground; fend off the attacker; refuse to give in; fight against; to oppose or withstand something."

Just as the offensive line of a football team plants their cleats in the turf to stand against the defense and protect the quarterback, so must believers take a stand to fend off the Enemy when he attacks. As believers, we must be able to identify who is out to get us if we are going to have a chance to win the fight. As 1 Peter 5:8 warns, *Be sober, be vigilant; because your adversary the devil walks about like a roaring lion, seeking whom he may devour.* Christian men must understand that they cannot afford to live careless, footloose or fancy-free lives because we have an enemy that forces us to stay alert.

> *Nonetheless, not only is it important to know when to resist the Devil but also how to resist him.*

The Devil is looking for opportunities to overwhelm men, using tricks and charm to tempt them. Often as men we don't know who the Enemy is or how he is coming at us. In turn, we don't know when to resist him. Nonetheless, not only is it important to know *when* to resist the Devil but also *how* to resist him.

Jesus gives us a great example in Matthew 4:1-11 of the way to defeat the Devil. The Word was His weapon when He resisted three temptations. If we Christian men are going to be able to take a solid stand against the slander, we must know the Word and use it on Satan whenever he comes knocking.

> *If we Christian men are going to be able to take a solid stand against the slander, we must know the Word and use it on Satan whenever he comes knocking.*

Jesus told Satan, "It is written"; therefore, he knew the Word. We discovered at this station that the reason so many of us fall is the lack of knowing God's Word intimately.

Too often, we men are guilty of depending on others such as pastors, teachers and wives to do all of our studying and praying for us. When the Enemy comes against us, we are not equipped, so we fall to his devices. Men, we can no longer devalue the Word of God, prayer or fellowship. If we continue do so, we will lose the battle every time. Paul said, *Put on the whole armor of God, that you may be able to stand against the wiles of the devil* (Ephesians 6:11 NKJV).

When following this plan, you must remember that this is a work station. This is not a station where you can afford to be lax; confession is what you are seeking. After confession has taken place, offer some helpful biblical solutions.

For example, in Christian Men Connect, every man was assigned a prayer partner. We then made sure every brother was held accountable. We vowed that we would become men under discipline and instruction to produce our spiritual maturity. We then concluded our session by falling on our knees and asking God for strength to be able to take a stand against the Devil because we knew he was coming to attack us.

**Reflect
and
Respond**

Ponder on this statement written by distinguished Chinese author and leader, Watchman Nee:

In order for a Christian to walk well before God, he must learn how to resist Satan. In order to do that, he must discern what is the work of Satan . . . If God's children are afraid of Satan, their portion will be defeat. On the other hand, let us not deceive ourselves into thinking that Satan will not attack us. He will assault—sometimes in our thought, sometimes in our body, sometimes in our spirit, and—sometimes in our environment. We will succumb to his attack only because of our foolishness. If we know our position and know that we are one with the Lord, and if we resist, he will flee from us. This resisting must be done in faith. Believe that he has fled, and he cannot but flee, for he has no ground to stand before the authority of God. We give thanks to God because He has given us the victory in Christ.

1. What tactic did Jesus use to defeat the Devil?

_____

_____

2. Are you prepared to counteract the Enemy's attack?

_____

_____

3. What Scripture passages can men use to combat the Devil when he comes?

_____

_____

4. Make a list of distractions that may prevent men from being alert to the Devil's entrapments.

_____

_____

5. How well do you know Satan? Are you able to recognize his devices?

_____

_____

Getting In Touch With God

—ᴡᴡ—

As for you, my son Solomon, know the God of your father, and serve Him with a loyal heart and with a willing mind; for the LORD searches all hearts and understands all the intent of the thoughts. If you seek Him, He will be found by you; but if you forsake Him, He will cast you off forever.
—I Chronicles 28:9 (NKJV)

Station Four: *Draw Closer To God*

Many Christian men feel as though God is so far away that they find it hard to experience His presence or power on a regular basis. Many will openly admit what they think about God and know of Him intellectually, but when it comes to a relationship of engaging with Him daily, something is dramatically wrong. There appears to be some type of disconnect. The relationship that God wants for His people involves an intimate knowledge of Him.

What would happen if we just talked with our wife and children once a day and did not spend any time with them? The relationship would die emotionally, the passionate fire would go out and the sparks would stop flying.

One major problem that we face as Christian men is not constantly making sure we cultivate our relationship with God. After we encounter Him at conversion, we start to feel

His power within and realize something has happened within our hearts. The experience is so powerful that we immediately start telling everyone the details. When we don't experience God daily, however, we fail to nurture our relationship with Him. That is when we fall to temptation and begin to feel distant from God.

This work station, "Draw Closer to God," is designed to help men renew or rekindle their relationship with God by drawing near to Him. As James 4:8 (NKJV) tells us, *Draw near to God and He will draw near to you.* As men, we must pursue an intimate love relationship with God.

The concept of drawing near to God was associated originally with the Levitical priests, as recorded in Exodus 19:22 and Leviticus 10:3. We can look at these verses to describe anyone's approach to God. It is imperative for Christian men to understand that salvation involves more than submitting to God and resisting the Devil. The redeemed heart longs for communion and fellowship with the lifter and lover of their hearts: God Almighty.

David knew God in a very personal way, but he, like many men, fell into sin. Although he messed up, he still had a desire to seek God. As we read in Psalm 63:10: *Oh, God, You* are *my God; early will I seek You; my soul thirsts for You; my flesh longs for You in a dry and thirsty land where there is no water.* David took the initiative to draw closer to God, and we, just like David, must be intentional about drawing close to Him as well.

What happens when we draw near to God or seek Him? He will draw near to us. That's mighty good news! I told you early on that God wants a relationship, not a casual commitment. God is just waiting to pour out His power in the lives of those who love Him and seek Him. Second Chronicles 15:2b says, *The LORD is with you while you are with Him. If you seek Him, He will be found by you; but if you forsake Him, He will forsake you.*

So what must we do in order to renew our relationship with God? Well, we must take the same steps we would with our wife and children in our attempt to repair the relationship. We need to apologize for not doing our part to keep the relationship fresh and strong, recommit ourselves and then fall in love all over again.

Again, the same principle works with God. He is just waiting for our call. Isaiah 55:6-7 reminds us:

> *Seek the LORD while He may be found,*
> *Call upon Him while He is near.*
> *Let the wicked forsake his way,*
> *And the unrighteous man his thoughts;*
> *Let him return to the LORD,*
> *And He will have mercy on him;*
> *And to our God,*
> *For He will abundantly pardon.*

This is great news for every man. You can have a one-on-one relationship with the Lord.

Station Four was powerful and enlightening. Once the importance of a true relationship with God was delivered, it was time to call upon Him. We began to share how we desperately needed and wanted to have a relationship with God. We bowed our knees and began to ask Him to renew us in His light.

God did more than what we asked. He poured out His power in a most unusual way. The men were crying, confessing their sins, and telling the Lord that they loved Him. They were thirsty for God and desperate for Him at the same time. The more cries rang out, the more God showed us that we were not alone.

One of the major problems with us Christian men is far too often we are not thirsty enough for the Lord's presence or power. During this station, however, God satisfied our thirst. We experienced Him in a mighty way. We could not deny that His awesome power was in our midst.

┌─────────────────┐
│   │
│ *Reflect*   │
│   *and*   │
│ *Respond*   │
│   │
└─────────────────┘

Just a closer walk with Thee,
Grant it, Jesus, is my plea,
Daily walking close to Thee,
Let it be, dear Lord, let it be.
I am weak, but Thou art strong;
Jesus, keep me from all wrong;
I'll be satisfied as long
As I walk, let me walk close to Thee.

(Writer Unknown)

1. Are you or the men you minister to walking in a close, intimate relationship with God?

_____

_____

2. Describe and discuss a time when you have not felt close to God.

_____

_____

3. What has kept you or men you know from having an intimate relationship with God?

_____

_____

4. Are you thirsty enough for the Lord's presence or power?

_____

_____

5. List several passages in the Bible that can be used to help men draw close to God.

_____

_____

Face It and God Will Fix It

—✺—

I acknowledged my sin to You, and my iniquity I have not hidden. I said, "I will confess my transgressions to the LORD," and You forgave the iniquity of my sin. —Psalm 32:5

Station Five: *Strongholds*

This station can stand alone as a book in itself. What it addresses is dealing with "strongholds." Let me encourage you not to rush through this station. Men need time to open up, ponder thoughts, cry, and reflect on past issues and painful situations. This station was designed to last for two days, but once the men at our spiritual boot camp started opening up, we ended up here for eight days.

They talked candidly and frankly about the pain, shame and blame they had been carrying for years. We shared testimony after testimony, confession after confession and tear after tear. Deliverance started taking place in a way that I can't even begin to explain. God's power was definitely working throughout our gathering.

The apostle Paul reminds us, *Though we walk in the flesh, we do not war after the flesh* (2 Corinthians 10:3). As Christians, we are engaged in intense warfare with a relentless enemy, the Devil. In Ephesians 2:2, he is called the prince of the power of the air. It is imperative that Christian men know the nature of the battle. Since the Devil and all of his forces are spirits, our battle is a spiritual one, so it must be treated as such.

We must realize that since we are in a fight, we must know our opponent. Often, as men we get so content and comfortable with our bondages, hang-ups, and handicaps that we learn how to function with our dysfunctionality. I, like so many others, realize that any form of bondage or stronghold in which a man becomes ensnared is not intentional: there is always a root cause.

> *Often, as men we get so content and comfortable with our bondages, hang-ups, and handicaps that we learn how to function with our dysfunctionality.*

Whenever we permit our strongholds to consume and take charge of us, any normal levels of restraint and self-control are removed. We rationalize our actions, paying no attention to the consequences and the damage that can be done to our character and reputation. The thrill of continuing to engage in the stronghold practically reaches a point of no return, and the entrapment begins.

We had several father-and-son teams attending this spiritual jubilee for men. One father got up to share about his past stronghold of pornography that had a grip on him for years. Although he came to church every Sunday, he was still watching pornographic movies. He told us that it kept him from going deeper in his spiritual walk with Christ. His pastor would ask him to take on responsibilities, but he wouldn't because of his stronghold and the guilt it caused, not to mention the shame. Praise God that he has been delivered for seven years and is now able to freely talk about it!

People, both in our past and present, can exert a tremendous amount of influence in our lives. Unfortunately, sometimes these individuals can push us in the wrong direction.

After the father finished his testimony, to our amazement, his son got up and began to share about his tussle with the same stronghold. He told his dad that he knew he had a problem with pornography.

Unfortunately, because pornography was available in the house, his son was exposed to it too, and he succumbed to the same temptation for years. He spoke of his struggles and how he had to fight this unclean spirit. The son went on to share how he also had surrendered his problem to Christ and that he had been clean for over two years. The father rose up and apologized to his son, and they shared a very emotionally moving embrace. Oh, what a God-moment!

Another brother got up to tell how he faced his stronghold. He talked about being an adulterer for over 14 years and how this sin had such a hold on him. He went on to share how he had lived a double life, managing two households for years all the while attending church. But he too came face to face with himself, his sin and God. He found freedom by confessing and then repenting from his sins. He had been delivered by none other than Jesus Christ.

Having said this, let's take a more in-depth look at the definition of the word "stronghold." According to Webster's Dictionary, a stronghold can be defined as "a fortified place; a place of security or survival; or a place dominated by a particular group or marked by a particular characteristic." The Greek-English Lexicon defines a stronghold as "a strong military fortification; a stronghold or fortress."

In a number of languages, the use of the word "stronghold" may be more satisfactorily rendered as a kind of simile to indicate a figurative usage, such as "powerful weapons with which to destroy false arguments in the same way that people would destroy fortresses." In some languages, a "fortress" may be described in terms of its function: "a place for protection" or "a place to defend oneself." Often, however, a fortress is described in terms of its construction, such as "a strong-walled place."

In 2 Corinthians 10:4, the word "stronghold" is used figuratively regarding the strength of false arguments. According to noted author, Jim Logan, a stronghold is "a mindset saturated with helplessness that causes one to accept it as unchangeable." As Christians, we know this is contrary to the will of God. It is this mindset that holds us hostage and leads us to believe we are hopelessly locked in a situation that we are powerless to change. Satan disguises himself so well and cunningly maneuvers his way into our lives so subtly that often we don't even see him coming. Then, before we know it, he has set up strongholds in our minds.

> *Hence, the battle begins in the mind, is fought in the mind and won in the mind.*

Second 2 Corinthians 10:5 tells us that Satan targets our minds. In this passage, Paul discusses speculations (NASB) and every high and lofty thing that rises up against the knowledge of God, along with our need to take every thought captive to the obedience of Christ. Think about it. Where do speculations come from? The mind. Where is knowledge rooted? The mind. Where do thoughts come from? The mind. It is all in the mind. Hence, the battle begins in the mind, is fought in the mind and won in the mind. Paul understood that the battle starts and ends in the mind. That's why in Ephesians he exhorted the believer to put on the helmet of salvation to protect his head.

> *Satan cannot build a stronghold unless we give him ground.*

The Devil is playing with our minds. He taps into our thoughts, influences our decisions and manipulates our words. It was the same way with Peter, who thought it was his own mind that told him to inform Jesus He could not die the way the Scriptures had prophesied. Jesus rebuked Satan because he knew it was him behind the thought.

> *If we are tempted to merely establish a truce with sin rather than eradicate it, sin will rise up against us in our moments of weakness.*

Remember the father mentioned earlier who struggled with pornography for many years? His mind held him hostage and made him feel like he was locked or trapped in this situation. What he failed to realize was that he had given Satan permission. Satan cannot build a stronghold unless we give him ground. Recall what Ephesians 4:27 asserts: *And do not give the devil an opportunity* (NASB). What this implies is to not allow the Devil a foothold, opening, opportunity or a place to set up shop in your life.

In *The Battle is the Lord's*, Tony Evans says that Satan wants to build a fortress in your mind; but he needs a piece of ground to build a stronghold, and he wants it to be permanent. Oh, but thanks be to God that we have weapons to help us defeat the Devil. By using our most powerful weapons — the Word, prayer, and reliance on the Holy Spirit — we can break free of any stronghold that has us bound. Glory, hallelujah! But it is imperative that we use our weapons.

When we became Christians, God declared war on every stronghold in our lives. Sinful behaviors and attitudes were firmly established in our character, but God commanded us to tear them down. The Holy Spirit pointed out areas of our lives that were and are opposed to God's will. If we

> *If there are strongholds in your life that you have never overcome, the Holy Spirit is still prepared to bring you into a state of complete victory.*

are tempted to merely establish a truce with sin rather than eradicate it, sin will rise up against us in our moments of weakness. In careless moments, these strongholds will tempt us to continue in our past sinful behaviors.

Do not underestimate the damaging power of sin. If there

are strongholds in your life that you have never overcome, the Holy Spirit is still prepared to bring you into a state of complete victory.

Overcoming Strongholds

How do I get started? How do I overcome or defeat my strongholds? These appear to be the most sought-after answers of the day. For many of us, life is up and down. We rise, and then we fall. Hopefully, the following steps will be essential in helping to provide viable solutions to these questions.

Step One: A great way to get started is to obey the Bible. Start by facing your sins. If you face your sin stronghold, God will fix it. Proverbs 28:13 says, *He that covereth his sins shall not prosper: but whoso confesseth and forsaketh them shall have mercy.* The only way to ensure gaining freedom from our strongholds is by facing them. We cannot afford to keep hiding our sins and think we are getting away with anything. Ask King David: the more he tried to cover up his sin, the worse he felt. Psalm 32:3 says, *When I kept silence, my bones waxed old through my roaring all the day long.* Stop beating yourself up, and face it!

Step Two: After we face our sins, we must confess them. Sin must not be covered, but confessed. 1 John 1:9 (NKJV) says, *If we confess our sins, He is faithful and just to forgive us our sins, and to cleanse us from all unrighteousness.* Continual confession of sin is an indication of genuine salvation. While false teachers would not admit their sins, the genuine Christians admitted and forsook them (Psalm 32:3-5). The term "confess" means to say the same thing about sin as God does. You must acknowledge His perspective about sin.

> *Confession is God's provision to clear away obstacles that hinder our relationship with God and others.*

Confession is God's provision to clear away obstacles that hinder our relationship with God and others. As men we have several hurdles to jump. That is why I believe in support groups. Men need a place where they can share openly. Confession is a command given to every Christian. James advised that when we sin, it is important for us to confess not only to God, but also to fellow Christians (James 5:16).

> *If true repentance does not come out of a confession, it is merely admission and not true confession.*

Confession among fellow believers is not practiced often in the church for many reasons. Contrary to those reasons, our group was able to see the power behind confessing our sins to one another. Now I know what you are thinking: What if someone shares the confession of others with those outside of the group? Again, we referred back to the covenant that was signed at the beginning of boot camp which clearly stated that you cannot repeat what is heard without permission. If the men disregarded the agreement, the consequence was removal from the group. There is a tremendous freedom that comes when one openly acknowledges the sinfulness of their actions to others without fear of exposure.

If true repentance does not come out of a confession, it is merely admission and not true confession. Remember that confession is not a sign of weakness; it is evidence of your refusal to allow sin to remain in your life—a mark of strength. It is important to confess our sins daily and specifically. Confession should not encompass or hide behind generalities.

After we confessed our sins and identified the strongholds, we wrote them down, put them in a box and vowed not to return to them again. We wrote a note to the Lord that read like this: "Dear Lord, you already know my sins. They are too heavy for me to carry, so here they are. Please take them. I give them to you in Jesus' name, Amen." We lined up one by one and dropped them in the box. Praise the Lord that many of the men here are still restraining themselves from going back to their strongholds.

Step Three: Remember to use *your* weapons. You cannot win the battle without them.

- *Ephesians 4:22: . . .that you put off, concerning your former conduct, the old man which grows corrupt according to the deceitful lusts, ...*
- *Ephesians 4:23: . . .and be renewed in the spirit of your mind, . . .*
- *Ephesians 4:24: . . .and that you put on the new man which was created according to God, in true righteousness and holiness.*

| **Reflect and Respond** | _____ |

We have an enemy. Satan has access to your life story; he knows what pathways you have traveled. It would be so much easier if the strongholds in our minds were simply the result of all the garbage we fed into our computer brains when we were growing up. If that were the case, we could simply reprogram our minds through Bible study, good counseling, and more education. Certainly, those three things are a big part of breaking down bondages. But there is more to the story. We have a spiritual enemy who acts like a computer "virus" seeking to gum up the whole works.

–Neil Anderson

1. What strongholds are you dealing with that you have not overcome? List them below.

_____

_____

2. John 8:36 says, "If the Son therefore shall make you free, ye shall be free indeed." Why is this simple verse so hard for men to accept and believe?

_____

_____

3. Write a note to the Lord, either by using the example given or by creating your own. Acknowledge and confess your sins and His ability to handle what you no longer can on your own. After writing it down and telling God about it, destroy the paper as a sign that you have laid aside that weight. Write down how that experience felt.

_____

_____

4. What steps are you willing to make to avoid falling into bondage again?

_____

_____

5. Identify a fellow Christian or Christian support group that you need to connect with and join to help keep you accountable and be a safe place for you to share confidential issues.

_____

_____

In It to Win It

—ൕ—

*Know ye not that they which run in a race run all, but one
receiveth the prize? So run, that ye may obtain.*
—I Corinthians 9:24

Station Six: *Laying Aside the Weight and Running the Race*

Station Six was devoted to laying aside the weight and running the race. This was a very encouraging station. By this time there was a spirit in the air that we could live victorious Christian lives as men. We shared Hebrews 12:1: *Therefore, since we have so great a cloud of witnesses surrounding us, let us also lay aside every encumbrance and the sin which so easily entangles us, and let us run with endurance the race that is set before us."* We discovered that people who live for God are not flawless or faultless; they are just faithful. As we took a look at the men and women of faith in Hebrew 11, we considered their lives and identified with their weaknesses. We were and are motivated to run the race.

Stop for a moment and choose a person in Chapter 11 that you can relate to. Maybe it is David or Gideon. What about Samson or Rahab? You make the choice. If they could make it to the Hall of Faith with God's help, we too can live a life pleasing to Him. If they could do it with their imperfect backgrounds, so can we. At this stage, the men were beginning to see that God is no respecter of persons, and He wants all of us to be faithful.

The deceased people of Chapter 11 give witness to the value and blessing of living by faith. Inspiration for running "the race" is not to receive praise from observing heavenly saints. Instead, the runner is inspired by the godly examples those saints set during their lives. The great crowd is not comprised of spectators but rather is made up of ones whose past lives of faith encourages others to live that way (MacArthur Study Bible notes).

> *As Christian men and fathers, we must be in the race to win.*

As Christian men and fathers, we must be in the race to win. Too many of us are just meandering or wandering through life. We must challenge ourselves to lay aside the weight that causes us to wander aimlessly or sit idly through life. The encumbrance weight differs from physical weight in that the encumbrance refers to the main burden weighing down the Hebrews, which was the Levitical system with its legalism. Physical weight, on the other hand, is represented by an athlete who would strip away every piece of unnecessary clothing before competing in a race.

As men of God we must remove those things that will keep us from effectively running the race. After completing this work station of the boot camp, we concluded that if we don't remove those things that hinder us, they can lead to sin or entanglement. Therefore, we must deal with the weight, whatever it may be.

> ## *Reflect and Respond*

Do you recall the story of David and Goliath? Remember when Saul gave David his armor and helmet to use to fight against Goliath? After David put on the armor, he found that it was too big and extremely heavy. It weighed David down. The armor suppressed his ability to freely move forward. David said he had not proved or tested them. In other words, he had not practiced, nor was he used to all that gear. It would become a hindrance and nuisance to him. Therefore, he had to lay aside the excess weight and use what he knew and was comfortable with to win the battle ahead.

What did David use? He used what was familiar to him. He relied on what would ensure his victory, which was more than just a slingshot and rocks. David's recollection of his past experience and triumphs with God on his side would solidify his victory. And so it is with us. If we are going to run the race to win, we must unload any excessive, unnecessary baggage that may hinder our progress and ability to win the battle. We must rely on what we know will ensure our victory, and that is our faith and trust in God.

1. What excess weight are you, or men that you know, carrying that has hindered or is hindering them from running the race to win?

_____

_____

2. What person mentioned in Hebrews 11 can you relate to, and why?

_____

_____

3. How can you encourage and challenge yourself and other men to get in the race and run it with determination to win?

_____

_____

4. Are you living the victorious Christian life? Discuss.

_____

_____

5. What plan of action do you have in place when obstacles come your way during the race that will keep you from becoming sidelined or disqualified?

_____

_____

Do You Love Him?

—ᴍ—

*Jesus answered and said to him, "If anyone loves Me, he will keep My word; and My Father will love him, and We will come to him and make Our home with him." —*John 14:23 (NKJV)

Station Seven: *Falling in Love with Jesus*

We had now reached the last station of our 21-day spiritual journey, which I termed "Falling in Love With Jesus." After we had cried, embraced and shared with one another, there was a bond that developed between us that was truly divine. As we reflected back on the past 20 days, the men shared their excitement about writing a vision statement for their families, a required assignment in which they asked their wives and children how they could pray for them.

One gentleman shared how he had been free from an addiction since the beginning of boot camp, and others mentioned how good they felt about their relationship with God. There was a spirit of freedom resting over the men that had not been present on Day One. The brothers had found hope, encouragement and tranquility. They had renewed their commitments, so they had become fired up and were ready to face the challenges ahead.

My biggest fear, however, was how they would fare after Christian Men Connect Boot Camp was over. Did they possess the spirit of Caleb? Would they be able to say that the Lord delighted in them? Would they be well able to keep their focus on Him in the days, months and years to come? What would be the key to preventing them from going back to their old habits and lifestyles? How could they keep their fire burning and their lights bright?

After pondering this, the Lord gave me John 14:21 (NKJV) to share with them: *"He who has My command-ments and keeps them, it is he who loves Me. And he who loves Me will be loved by My Father, and I will love him and manifest Myself to him."* What would it take? It would require a genuine and sincere love for the Lord Jesus Christ, which would keep the men faithful to His Word and prevent them from going back to their old habits and ways they had renounced.

> *When there is a struggle to obey God, that is usually a sign or indication that our hearts have wandered from Him.*

In this passage of John, Jesus emphasized the need for the habitual practice of obedience to His commands as evidence of the believer's love for Him and the Father. Obedience to God's commands must come from our hearts. When there is a struggle to obey God, that is usually a sign or indication that our hearts have wandered from Him. Many will proclaim their love for God but at the same time express difficulty in obeying Him in certain areas of their lives.

> *He is not satisfied with occasional love or partial obedience; never assume that He is.*

The goal of this last station was to help us understand that God wants our love and obedience every day. If I told my wife I loved her at certain times and then strug-gled to love her at others, my rela-tionship with her would be in jeopardy. She would question my sincerity because she wants my love at all times. This is the same with God. He is not satisfied with occasional love or partial obedience; never assume that He is.

> *God's love for us is unconditional, no matter what condition or state we find ourselves; however, we must continually examine our love for Him.*

I found out during our period of sharing that many of the men felt like failures because they had committed sin in their lives. They were reminded that there was none righteous, no, not one. All of us had lost focus and disobeyed God at some point in life. There was a constant reminder to the men that sin does not stop God from loving us. When we disobey His Word, it grieves Him, but He still loves us. Even when we deny Him by the way we live, He still loves us. God's love for us is unconditional, no matter what condition or state we find ourselves; however, we must continually examine our love for Him. Peter is a good example of this.

Peter miserably failed the Lord when he fled with the other disciples from the Garden of Gethsemane, later denying that he ever knew Jesus. Peter must have wondered, like most of us at times, if he was even worthy of being one of Jesus' disciples. This is the sentiment the men in our boot camp shared. They didn't feel God could use them because of their past and present sin. The men were reassured that, just as Jesus took Peter aside and spoke with him, He would do the same with them.

Thankfully, Jesus doesn't beat us down with His Word, knock us down with His hand, let us down by leaving us alone or make us feel guilty. Nor will He humiliate us like so many others do. He will simply ask us to examine our love for Him. He asked Peter a very simple question: "Do you love Me?" That's what He's asking all of us: "Do you love Me?" If we can answer "Yes, Lord" like Peter, He will reaffirm His will for our life and restore us to our responsibilities.

| Reflect and Respond | _____ |

Meditate on these lyrics. Do you believe them to be true? Does your life reflect it?
Falling in love with Jesus

Falling in love with Jesus
Falling in love with Jesus
Was the best thing I've ever done.
In His arms, I feel protected.
In His arms, never disconnected.
In his arms, I feel protected.
There's no place I'd rather be.

—Jonathan K. Butler

1. What do you believe keeps Christian men from going back to their old lifestyles and habits?

_____

_____

2. How would you rate your love life with Christ?

_____

_____

3. Do you believe in the power of God's love for you in spite of you? Discuss.

_____

_____

4. Do you struggle with obeying God in a particular area of your life? Why is it harder for you to obey in that area?

_____

_____

5. If Jesus were to ask you right now, "Do you love me?" what would your response be?

_____

_____

Little Becomes Much

—ᘓᘓ—

Then He took the five loaves and the two fish, and looking
up to heaven, He blessed and broke them, and gave them to the
disciples to set before the multitude. So they all ate and were
filled, and twelve baskets of the leftover fragments were
taken up by them. —Luke 9:16-17 (NKJV)

History is filled with men who have made small changes
that have greatly impacted our society and world.
George Washington Carver, who discovered over 300 uses
for the peanut and hundreds of uses for the soybean, pecan
and sweet potato, made a small change with crops and the
agricultural system which led to a great impact and improve-
ment in America's economy. Always crediting God, he willingly gave his discoveries to mankind, completely changing
the South's agricultural industry. He even donated his
life's earnings to the establishment of the Carver Research
Foundation at Tuskegee Institute for the continuing research
in agriculture. His great impact led to this inscription on his
grave: "He could have added fortune to fame, but caring for
neither, he found happiness and honor in being helpful to
the world."

Then there's Benjamin Franklin. Many believe him to be
the father of electricity. His kite experiment established the
relationship between lightning and electricity. This *sparking*

relationship led to the invention of the lightning rod, which brought him international fame and opened the path to modern advancements in electricity. What impact!

How could we forget the famous inventor, scientist and innovator, Alexander Graham Bell? Influenced by his mother's and wife's inability to hear, he experimented with hearing devices, and that led him to patent the telephone. Who would have ever thought that his small invention to help his loved ones would become the mega- telecommunications phenomenon that it is today?

The Bible is filled with ordinary men who made a great impact. These men believed in God enough to act upon His Word. Remember Noah, who trusted God enough to build an ark on dry land that would be used to house and preserve a small remnant of people and animals? Those on the ark would help to repopulate the world after the massive flood that destroyed everyone else. *Impact.* How about Joseph, who would rise from a pit-and-prison experience and be set over all the land of Egypt to be honored as the means of saving countless human lives? *Impact.* What about Joshua? Joshua made a small investment and the walls of Jericho came down. He then led Israel over the Jordan, taking possession of the Promised Land. *Impact.*

If we men would just make a small change in our lives, we can bring down walls in our lives as well: walls of low self-esteem, walls of pride, walls of prejudice, walls of lies, walls of separation, walls of vain imaginations, walls of excuses and walls of frustration. The men mentioned above made a small change that had great impact. Are you willing to do the same? If so, face your pain, confess the blame and claim your change in Jesus' name!

I hope you have envisioned a portion of what occurred during our life-changing 21-day spiritual boot camp, Christian Men Connect. Paul reminds us in Philippians 4:13 that we can do all things through Christ who strengthens us. Make a small change today in your life, and I promise that you will become a better person in this life and the life to come.

You are probably asking yourself, how does one keep the momentum going at the conclusion of a 21-day boot camp? Well, get ready! The journey doesn't end here. We made a commitment to meet at 5:45 a.m. once a month to help hold one another accountable and encourage continued spiritual growth. Again, the journey does not end here. This phenomenal movement is designed to dwell within you at all times.

If you are a leader of men, why not take your men through this 21-day journey of deliverance? It's worth the investment—for yourself and others. Your little change can develop into so much, which can lead to an impact far greater than you could ever imagine. Start now by making a small change, and see what God will do with the rest. Be encouraged, my brother, and be blessed. Go, and impact!

Ordinary People

Just ordinary people
God uses ordinary people
He chooses people just like me and you
Who are willing to do as He commands
God uses people that will give Him all
No matter how small your all may seem to you
Because little becomes much as you place it in
the Master's hand.
Just ordinary people
My God uses ordinary people He chooses people
just like me and you
Who are willing, willing to do everything
that He commands
God uses people that will give Him all
No matter how small your all might seem to you
Because little becomes much as you place it
in the Master's hand.
Just like that little lad
Who gave Jesus all he had
How the multitude was fed
With the fish and the loaves of bread
What you have may not seem much
But when you yield it to the touch
Of the Master's loving hand, yes,
Then you'll understand how your life could
never be the same.

-Danniebelle Hall

Boot Camp Word of the Day

—ᠬᠤ—

Each day, meditate on the Word of the day and the Scripture passage that goes with it. Apply it daily and see the change it will make. This was a daily regime with the men as they memorized these passages during the 21-day journey of deliverance.

Chosen	John 15:16
Do Not Sin!	Psalms 119:11
Confess Your Faults!	James 5:16
Grow Up!	1 Peter 2:2
Make No Provisions!	Romans 13:14
Seek or Forsake!	2 Chronicles 15:2
Humble Yourself	Luke 14:11
You Can Do It!	Philippians 4:13
Be Cleansed!	1 John 1:9

Walk In the Spirit!	Galatians 5:16
Guard Your Heart!	Proverbs 4:23
Do Good!	James 4:17
God's Grace!	Titus 2:11
God Will Not Tempt You!	James 1:13
Are You Pleasing God?	2 Timothy 2:4
Spiritual Warfare!	2 Corinthians 10:3
The Real Enemy	Ephesians 6:12
Strongholds!	2 Corinthians 10:4
Prayer	1 Thessalonians 5:17
Seek God First!	Matthew 6:33
In It To Win It!	1 Corinthians 9:24

Works Cited

—ɷ—

Anderson, N. T. (1995). *Purity under Pressure : Making Decisions You Can Live with, Friendships, Dating, and Relationships That Last.* New York, NY: Harvest House.

Butler, J. 2004. The Worship Project on *Falling in Love with Jesus* [CD]. Maranatha! Music.

Cass, C. (2004, May 8). 1 of every 75 U.S. Men in Prison. In *CommonDreams.org.* Retrieved July 13, 2008, from http://www.commondreams.org/headlines04/0528-02.htm

Church on the Rock New Haven. (n.d.). Retrieved April 13, 2008, from http://www.rocknewhaven.org/male_statistics.htm

The Daily Motivator. (2005, June 18). Retrieved March 8, 2008, from http://greatday.com/motivate/050618.html

Evans, T. (2002). *The Battle Is the Lord's : Waging Victorious Spiritual Warfare.* New York: Moody.

Experiencing God Day by Day : A Devotional and Journal. (1997). New York, TN: B&H Group.

Hall, D. 1977. Ordinary People. On *Ordinary People* [CD]. Birdwing Music.

Logan, J. (Ed.). (1995). *Reclaiming Surrendered Ground : Protecting Your Family from Spiritual Attacks.* New York: Moody.

MacArthur, J. F. (Ed.). (1997). *The MacArthur Study Bible.* Carlisle: STL.

National Center for Health Statistics. (2007, October 31). Retrieved June 8, 2008, from http://www.cdc.gov/nchs/fastats/divorce.htm

U. (n.d.). Just a Closer Walk with Thee. On *Just a Closer Walk With Thee* [CD].

US. US Dept of Health & Human Services. Administration for Children & Families. (2006, May). *Healthy Marriage Initiative.* Retrieved April 8, 2008, from http://www.acf.hhs.gov/

Vital Statistics. (n.d.). In *Until There's a Cure.* Retrieved July 13, 2008, from http://www.until.org/statistics.shtml?gclid=cjhzy67fpjucfsxnigodefn7ag

Watchman, N. (n.d.). Resist the Devil. In *Two Listerners.* Retrieved May 24, 2008, from http://www.twolisteners.org/resist_the_devil.htm

CPSIA information can be obtained at www.ICGtesting.com
Printed in the USA
LVOW12s2001210814

400302LV00004B/5/P